Praise for
The Sign of the Cross

"Readers . . . will find Ghezzi's combination of biblical scholarship, church tradition, and common sense both informative and appealing."
—*Publishers Weekly*

"In this helpful resource, Bert Ghezzi, a Catholic writer, discusses the meaning of making the sign of the cross according to Scripture, church teaching, the writings of the church fathers, the testimony of the saints, theology books, and his own personal experience."
—*Spirituality & Health*

"His insights into spiritual life . . . and his enthusiasm for this 'easy spiritual discipline' may prove to be contagious—powerfully so."
—*First Things: A Journal of Religion, Culture, and Public Life*

"Using scripture, church teachings and his own prayer life, Ghezzi describes how the sign offers an opening to God, a renewal of baptism, a mark of discipleship, an acceptance of suffering, a defense against the devil, and a victory over self-indulgence."
—*Notre Dame Magazine,* pick of the week, May 3, 2004

"Ghezzi has placed the jewel of the prayer of the sign of the cross in a setting that reveals its beauty, inspiration, and holy energy."
—**Father Alfred McBride, O.Praem.,** author of *Essentials of the Faith* and *Images of Jesus*

"This slender volume calls Christians to a deeper awareness of what they are doing when they make this sign."
—*Review for Religious*

OTHER BOOKS BY BERT GHEZZI

Mystics and Miracles:
True Stories of Lives Touched by God

Voices of the Saints: A 365-Day
Journey with Our Spiritual Companions

Sacred Passages: Bringing the Sacraments to Life

The New Jerusalem Bible: Saints Devotional Edition

Getting Free: How to Overcome
Persistent Personal Problems

Being Catholic Today: Your Personal Guide

Guiltless Catholic Parenting from A to Y

Keeping Your Kids Catholic

THE SIGN OF THE CROSS

OF THE

CROSS

Recovering the Power
of the
Ancient Prayer

BERT GHEZZI

LOYOLAPRESS.
A JESUIT MINISTRY
Chicago

LOYOLA PRESS.
A JESUIT MINISTRY

3441 N. Ashland Avenue
Chicago, Illinois 60657
(800) 621-1008
www.loyolapress.com

Jacket and interior design by Megan Duffy Rostan
Cover photo: © CORBIS

Library of Congress Cataloging-in-Publication Data
Ghezzi, Bert.
   The sign of the cross: recovering the power of the ancient prayer / Bert Ghezzi.
      p. cm.
Includes bibliographical references.
   ISBN 0-8294-1619-6
   1. Cross, Sign of the. 2. Prayer. I. Title.
BV197.S5G48 2004
242'.72—dc22

                                                            2003020273

paperback ISBN-13: 978-0-8294-2166-8; ISBN-10: 0-8294-2166-1

Printed in the United States of America
LSC 2017

Infinite Wisdom has chosen the cross because a slight motion of the hand is sufficient to trace upon us the instrument of the divine torture—the bright and powerful sign that teaches us all that we have to know and serves as a shield against our enemies.

Blessed Alcuin (ca. 730–804)

For Richard and Patricia Easton

CONTENTS

INTRODUCTION
Recovering the Power of the Ancient Sign   1

1. A Short History of the Sign of the Cross   17

2. An Opening to God   27

3. A Renewal of Baptism   41

4. A Mark of Discipleship   55

5. An Acceptance of Suffering   69

6. A Defense against the Devil   79

7. A Victory over Self-Indulgence   91

CONCLUSION
Graces and Choices   103

Notes   111
Bibliography   117
Acknowledgments   119

Recovering the Power of the Ancient Sign

But as for me, it is out of the question that I should boast at all, except of the cross of our Lord Jesus Christ, through whom the world has been crucified to me, and I to the world. . . .

After this, let no one trouble me; I carry branded on my body the marks of Jesus.

Galatians 6:14, 17

⁓

This sign is a powerful protection. It is gratuitous, because of the poor. Easy because of the weak. A benefit from God, the standard of the faithful, the terror of demons.

St. Cyril of Jerusalem (ca. 317–86)[1]

⁓

Adorn and protect each of your members with this victorious sign, and nothing can injure you.

St. Ephraem of Syria (ca. 306–73)[2]

ALEXANDER SOLZHENITSYN leaned on his shovel and watched the gray clouds drag sullenly across the sky. A merciless wind tore at him through his prison garb. He felt as though it penetrated to his soul. Every one of his bones and muscles ached. Hunger gnawed his stomach. Years of hard labor in the Siberian work camp had ruined his health and stripped him of hope.

Solzhenitsyn could endure no longer. He dropped his shovel, left the work gang, and sat on a bench nearby. Soon a guard would command him to return to work. When he would ignore the order, the guard would beat him to death with his own shovel. He had seen it happen to others many times. *A quick, bloody death today,* thought Solzhenitsyn, *would be better than a slow death in a bleak, empty future.*

He stared at the ground, waiting for the inevitable. Soon he heard footsteps and braced himself in anticipation of the guard's harsh words. But when he raised his eyes, instead of a guard he saw a gaunt, elderly prisoner standing before him. The old man said nothing but knelt in front of Solzhenitsyn. With a stick he scratched the sign of the cross in the dirt and then hurried back to work.

Solzhenitsyn looked at the cross, and as he reflected on it, a ray of light penetrated his dark thoughts. In that moment his perspective changed radically. He realized that he did not have to face the evil of the gulag and the Soviets on his own diminished strength. With the power of the cross, he could withstand the evil of not one but a thousand Soviet empires.

He got up from the bench and returned to work. Although the record does not say so, I think that he must also have traced the ancient sign on his breast. None of Solzhenitsyn's external circumstances changed that day, but internally he had experienced a gentle revolution. The sign of the cross had blessed him with the grace of hope.[3]

I found this story in an Internet search, and it moved me deeply because it affirmed something I had been discovering in my prayer life. In the past few years I had taken the sign of the cross more seriously. I signed myself more frequently and with more reverence and faith. I sensed that in crossing myself I was tapping into a powerful divine energy that had many practical consequences for my life. It released graces that strengthened me to face the challenges that arose every day.

When I reflected on how things were going for me, I realized that I was doing a better job of controlling my anger and overcoming other problems. I also felt that I was relating to God more freely. I asked myself what I was doing differently that might account for this noticeable progress. The only answer I could come up with was my praying more earnestly with the sign of the cross.

As I sought to understand what was happening to me, I read some articles and books about the sign of the cross. A little research showed that what was a novel experience for me had been the normal, everyday experience of Christians in the Church's first centuries. Many of the early Christian writers described how believers signed themselves frequently. For example, Tertullian (ca. 160–ca. 225), a theologian writing at the turn of the third century, said, "In all our travels and movements, in all our coming in and going out, in putting on our shoes, at the bath, at the table, in lighting our candles, in lying down, in sitting down, whatever employment occupies us, we mark our foreheads with the sign of the cross."[4] My reading showed further that the Fathers of the Church testified to the great blessings and power afforded by the sign of the cross. I will quote the Fathers extensively throughout this book, but here I will cite only St. John Chrysostom (ca. 347–407), the eloquent fourth-century preacher and patriarch of Constantinople:

> Never leave your house without making the sign of the cross. It will be to you a staff, a weapon, an impregnable fortress. Neither man nor demon will dare to attack you, seeing you covered with such powerful armor. Let this sign teach you that you are a soldier, ready to combat against the demons, and ready to fight for the crown of justice. Are you ignorant of what the cross has done? It has vanquished death, destroyed sin, emptied hell, dethroned Satan, and restored the universe. Would you then doubt its power?[5]

Chrysostom's words about the sign of the cross are ever-green. His promises about its power for deliverance from evil, offensive and defensive spiritual warfare, spiritual support and freedom, and restoration hold true for us today.

An Invitation

When I was a boy my mother taught me to make the sign of the cross as I knelt for my prayers at bedtime. For all the years since then I have signed myself at the start and close of my prayers. But in retrospect I realize that, while I have always done it respectfully, until lately I did it routinely, superficially, and unaware of its significance. My recent experience has changed my view of the sign of the cross and my practice of it. I feel that I have recovered the tremendous power of this most ancient Christian prayer.

Sometimes as I sign myself I imagine that I have traveled back in time to Calvary. With Mary, Mary Magdalen, and John, I stand at the foot of the cross as a witness to the Lord's supreme sacrifice. I watch him die a horrific death out of love for me. Then a soldier pierces his side and a flood of graces flows from his heart. I am engulfed in unimaginable blessings. With this book I encourage you to join me at his cross. Come with me to Golgotha, where you also will discover the life-transforming power of the holy gesture and open yourself more fully to its wonderful graces.

I invite you to explore with me the multidimensional realities of the sign of the cross. If you accept—and I hope you do, for I know you won't regret it—you too will receive its immeasurable blessings.

If you are like me, you are not satisfied with books about spirituality that aim merely to increase your knowledge. You desire something more. You want experience that touches your heart. You long for realities that address your deepest yearnings. This little book will increase your knowledge of the sign of the cross so you can make it more intelligently. And as you make the sign with more understanding, it will also expand your experience of God and energize your spirit.

I have discovered six dynamic truths about the sign of the cross that I derived from insights I found in Scripture, Church teaching, the writings of the Fathers of the Church, the testimony of the saints, theology books, and the personal experiences of mine and my friends'. Each of the six exposes extraordinary facets of the spiritual life that God gives us as our way to happiness. I offer them to you in successive chapters, beginning with chapter 2.

No empty gesture, the sign of the cross is a potent prayer that engages the Holy Spirit as the divine advocate and agent of our successful Christian living. When we trace it on our body, it stirs up the new life of the Spirit that we received in baptism and vitalizes our prayer by drawing us closer to God. Making the sign affirms our decision to follow Christ, allowing him to assume our burdens and free us to live joyfully. The sign of the cross is also a practical tool for dealing with problems. It invites Christ to support us in our pain and suffering and works handily to defuse our worst inclinations and to dispel the temptations of the devil. And the sign is much more, for with a slight motion of the hand and a few simple words it sums up the truth and power of the Christian life.

A Fount of Blessing

My enthusiasm for the sign of the cross coupled with the enthusiasm of the early Christian writers may lead you to a false conclusion about how it works. Let's be clear up front that the gesture does not *cause* blessing or empowerment. Rather the sign of the cross *opens us* to receiving God's blessing and power. Distinguishing sacramentals from sacraments will help to explain this.

The Church calls the sign of the cross a sacramental because it is like a sacrament. Sacramentals and sacraments work toward the same end, but they differ in a fundamental way. A sacrament is a sign or symbol that causes what it signifies. For example, in the Eucharist God uses bread and wine to make Christ's body and blood truly present on our altars. So a sacrament is an outward sign of inward grace. A sacramental, on the other hand, does not directly confer divine grace; rather it prepares us to receive God's blessing and disposes us to cooperate with it. While it does not cause grace, it does touch us with spiritual power that it receives from the prayer of the Christian community. "Sacramentals," says the *Catechism of the Catholic Church*, "signify effects, particularly of a spiritual nature, which are obtained through the intercession of the Church."[6] Throughout the world during Mass and the Liturgy of the Hours, in chapels and private homes, and in all places, members of the Body of Christ pray fervently for family and friends. There is great power in this prayer of the Church, and the person who prays in conjunction with a sacramental connects with its spiritual energy—an activity akin to plugging an appliance into an electrical outlet and flipping on the switch. So when we make the sign of the cross prayerfully, we "plug into" a source of spiritual power generated by the intercession of all the members of the Body of Christ.

Every time we make the sign of the cross, we invite the Lord to bless us, and he always responds. We may sense his action as Solzhenitsyn did when he recovered hope. But most often when we make it, we don't feel anything. That's because God is using the movements of our body to reach our spirit, and our senses cannot detect much of what he does there. Yet each time we cross ourselves, something significant happens within us. The Lord gives us a new burst of divine energy. When we touch our forehead, breast, and shoulders in his name, he touches our spirit with the blessings of the cross.

The Church uses the word *grace* to describe the blessing bestowed on us through the sacraments and sacramentals. *Grace* refers to an outpouring of the Holy Spirit that comes to us as God's free gift. *Sanctifying grace* is the presence of the Spirit that was bestowed on us at our baptism and that saves us and makes us holy. *Actual grace* refers to a specific gift of divine energy that supports our Christian life. Solzhenitsyn, for example, abided in the sanctifying grace that flooded him at his baptism, and the divine intervention that gave him hope to endure the gulag was an actual grace.

Like all sacramentals, the sign of the cross disposes us to make better use of sanctifying grace and calls on God to give us actual graces. The *Catechism* emphasizes this reality:

> For well-disposed members of the faithful, the liturgy of the sacraments and sacramentals sanctifies almost every event of their lives with the divine grace which flows from the Paschal mystery of the Passion, Death, and Resurrection of Christ. From this source all sacraments and sacramentals draw their power. There is scarcely any proper use of material things which cannot be thus directed toward the sanctification of men and the praise of God.[7]

Here the *Catechism* recommends the ancient Christian practice of consecrating daily life with sacramentals, the chief of which is the sign of the cross. Invoking the blessing of the sign during the ordinary activities of our day elevates them to opportunities for drawing nearer to God—activities such as waking up, eating, driving the children to school, starting the workday, responding to e-mail, shopping, relaxing with family, and going to bed.

Blessing others and objects with the sign of the cross is another ancient Christian practice. We make the sign in the air over a person or thing while calling on the name of the Father, the Son, and the Holy Spirit. The Church extensively employs this form of the sign of the cross as a blessing in the liturgy. During Mass, for example, the presider makes the sign over the bread and wine to prepare them for the sacrifice, and at the end of Mass, he signs a blessing over the people to strengthen them for their service of God and others.

The Church also encourages laypeople to use the sign of the cross to bless others: children, spouses, pregnant women, friends, guests, and so on. And we bless things with it—such as homes, cars, tools, and food—so that our use of them may open us more fully to God.

With this gesture we help others dispose themselves to receive the power Christ released for them from his cross. Striking evidence of this comes from the lives of the saints. Many brought God's healing to the sick by blessing them with the sign of the cross. Once, for example, St. Clare of Assisi (ca. 1193–1253) walked into her convent's infirmary, made the sign five times, and five of her sisters were instantly cured of their illnesses. St. Vincent Ferrer (ca. 1350–1419) regularly blessed crowds of thousands with his hand-held cross, and hundreds were healed.[8] Mary Lou, my wife, and I make no claims to sainthood, but when our seven children were ill we prayed for them with the sign of the cross and often saw them recover more quickly than medical science predicted they would. (Of course, we also took them to our family physician and gave them their medicine.)

A Simple Gesture and a Simple Prayer

I find it difficult to apply the recommendations of many spiritual books. They overwhelm me with recipes of 7, 12, or 144 things that I must do to achieve spiritual success or with complex programs of spiritual disciplines that require more effort than I can muster. While I admire the wisdom of such books, I am rarely able to do what they suggest. You may feel the same way. But following the advice I give in this little book requires only the effort of making a simple gesture and praying a simple prayer. Christ did the hard work when he endured his excruciating passion and death and made his cross a fount of blessing for us. You can start right now to enjoy more fully the blessings and power of this ancient sign. Just trace it on your body with reverence and faith. Go ahead, do it—even if you are reading in a public place.

Before we consider together the six truths that will broaden your understanding and experience of the sign of the cross, I want to show how Christians have made it in the past and how we have come to make the large and little signs that we make today.

ONE

A Short History of the Sign of the Cross

Go . . . all through Jerusalem, and mark a cross on the foreheads of all who grieve and lament over all the loathsome practices in it.

Ezekiel 9:4

And then you bless yourself with the sign of the holy cross. . . . And in this blessing you begin with your hand from the head downward, and then to the left side and after to the right side, in token and belief that Our Lord Jesus Christ came down from the head, that is from the Father into the earth by his holy Incarnation, and from the earth into the left side, that is hell, by his bitter Passion, and from thence unto his Father's right side by his glorious Ascension.

Mirror of Our Lady (fifteenth century)[1]

As soon as you get out of bed in the morning, you should bless yourself with the sign of the Holy Cross and say: "May the will of God, the Father, the Son and the Holy Spirit be done! Amen."

Martin Luther, *The Small Catechism*[2]

D URING THE REFORMATION of the sixteenth century some Protestants repudiated the sign of the cross because they judged it to be superstitious. No doubt the practice of some Catholics had given them cause for this conclusion. As early as the sixth century, the misuse of the sign was drawing criticism from leaders in the Church. For example, St. Caesarius (ca. 470–543), the bishop of Arles and one of Christianity's first bestselling authors, rebuked those who signed themselves while on their way to steal or commit adultery.[3] Closer to home, you and I may have unknowingly made a superstitious use of the sign when we wished friends good luck by telling them we would keep our fingers crossed. But Martin Luther himself did not abandon the sign of the cross—in fact, he recommended it in his *Small Catechism* in an appendix on family prayer.

No trace of superstition or magic marred the sign of the cross in its origins. While no direct evidence exists, it seems clear from circumstances that the holy gesture had its roots as a prayer in apostolic times. Fourth-century Father of the Church St. Basil (ca. 329–79) said that the apostles "taught us to mark with the sign of the cross those who put their hope in the Lord,"[4] that is, those who presented themselves for baptism.

So early Christians probably learned to make the sign of the cross at their baptism when the celebrant marked them with it to claim them for Christ. There is some evidence for this in Scripture. For example, St. Paul reminded the Ephesians that they had received the sign at baptism when he said, "You have been stamped with the seal of the Holy Spirit of the Promise" (Ephesians 1:13). And Paul may have been speaking of his being signed with the cross at baptism when he told the Galatians, "I carry branded on my body the marks of Jesus" (Galatians 6:17). I will say more about this later, but for now I merely want to show that the sign of the cross originated among people who were not far removed from Christ himself.

By the third century, Christians commonly used a thumb or index finger to trace a little cross on their forehead. They

associated the practice with references in Ezekiel 9:4 and
Revelation 7:3, 9:4, and 14:1, all of which describe believers
signing God's seal on their forehead.[5] They also traced the
little sign on their lips and breast, as we still do today when
the Gospel is announced at Mass. And they made the sign
in the air as a blessing over people and things. Tertullian,
for example, told of a woman who signed her bed,[6] and St.
Cyril of Jerusalem described Christians tracing the cross
"over the bread we eat and the cups we drink." Using the
sign of the cross as a blessing may have prompted some
Christians to make the larger sign that we know today, but
that practice did not come into common use until later.

Opposition to the Monophysite heresy in the seventh and
eighth centuries may have contributed to the popularization
of the larger sign. To summarily refute these heretics—who
held that Christ had only one nature, which was divine,
instead of two natures, one human and one divine—
Catholics in the East began to sign themselves with two
fingers or with a thumb and forefinger. They had to trace
a larger sign over their body so that their use of two fingers
to defend the truth would be visible to all. Imagine the duel
that occurred when a Catholic encountered a Monophysite.
The Catholic would conspicuously make a large sign with

two fingers and then hurry to the other side of the street. The Monophysite would respond by making a large sign with his index finger and then walk off in a huff. The idea of that scene may make us smile, but in those days ordinary folks' tempers flared over theological issues.

By the ninth century, Christians in the East were making the larger gesture with their thumb and two fingers displayed, symbolizing the Trinity, and with their ring finger and little finger folded in, symbolizing Christ's two natures. Typically, they touched their forehead and moved to their breast, then crossed their shoulders from right to left. The large right sign of the cross came to be the common practice in the Eastern Church.

How Western Christians came to adopt the larger sign of the cross is less clear. Apparently after the ninth century some Western Christians were imitating the practice of the Eastern Church and were signing themselves with a large right cross. But at the same time others in the West had begun to trace the large cross over their breast by moving their hand from their left shoulder to their right shoulder.

Innocent III (ca. 1160–1216), who was pope at the beginning of the thirteenth century, directed Christians to sign themselves with two fingers and thumb extended, indicating no preference for either the right cross or the left. But before the end of the Middle Ages, Western Christians favored the large left cross. For example, the *Mirror of Our Lady,* a late-fifteenth-century document, taught the Brigittine Sisters of Syon Abbey, Middlesex, England, to cross themselves from left to right. It explained that the movement from forehead to breast meant that Christ came down from heaven to earth in his incarnation. And the movement from the left to right shoulder indicated that Christ at his death descended into hell and then ascended to heaven to sit at the Father's right hand.

By the end of the Middle Ages—probably under the extensive influence of Benedictine monasteries, where the practice was to make a large left cross with an open hand—most Western Christians were making the sign of the cross as many of us do today.

In every age Christians commonly, but not indispensably, accompanied the act of making the sign with words of prayer. The prayers themselves varied greatly. In the earliest centuries, they used invocations like "The sign of Christ," "The seal of the living God," and "In the name of Jesus." In later ages they prayed, "In the name of Jesus of Nazareth," "In the name of the Holy Trinity," and "In the name of the Father, and of the Son, and of the Holy Spirit," the latter being the most common prayer that we use today. Christians have also used formulas suggested by the liturgy, such as "O God, come to my assistance" and "Our help is in the name of the Lord."[7] This diversity of words that can accompany the sign should encourage you to pray spontaneously when you cross yourself, a practice that I recommend in later chapters.

Twenty-first-century Christians have inherited a variety of ways to make the sign. Today you will see people marking themselves with large left crosses or large right crosses; with an open hand or with two fingers and thumb extended; tracing little crosses on their forehead, lips, and breast with one finger, two fingers, or thumb and forefinger. You may see a Hispanic youth make a large left cross and then kiss a little cross made with thumb and forefinger, a common practice among Catholics of Latin American descent. You will see clerics in liturgical settings and laypeople in ordinary situations blessing people and objects with two fingers and a thumb or with an open hand. But no matter how they do it—large or small; with one finger, two fingers, three fingers, or an open hand—all who sign themselves with faith are presenting themselves to the Lord.

Now we will begin our quest to recover the power of this ancient prayer, first examining how the sign opens us to God.

TWO

An Opening to God

Whatever you say or do, let it be in the name of the Lord Jesus, in thanksgiving to God the Father through him.

Colossians 3:17

❦

Whatever you ask in my name I will do,
so that the Father may be glorified in the Son.
If you ask me anything in my name,
I will do it.

John 14:13–14

❦

When you sign yourself, think of all the mysteries contained in the cross. It is not enough to form it with the finger. You must first make it with faith and good will. . . . When you mark your breast, your eyes, and all your members with the sign of the cross, offer yourself as a victim pleasing to God.

St. John Chrysostom[1]

SOMETIMES CHRISTIANS make the sign of the cross without saying any words. For example, I silently mark myself when I board an aging airplane or cross the street at a busy intersection, acting on the ancient belief that the sign wards off danger.

But while tracing the sign on our body we usually say, "In the name of the Father, and of the Son, and of the Holy Spirit. Amen." We call on the Lord in this way especially when we begin and end our prayers. That's how the Christian community starts its celebration of the greatest prayer of the Church. And Mass always ends with the priest's pronouncing these words in his cruciform blessing of the assembly.

Making the sign with the invocation of the Trinity has a multilevel spiritual significance. On one level, it serves as a minicreed that we can frequently use to affirm our faith. On another level, it corrects our misimpressions of God and welcomes us into the presence of the Trinity. And on still another, it elevates our prayer, allowing us to pray with Godpower instead of mere humanpower.

Consider these realities with me. Reflecting on them will change the way you make the sign of the cross and will consequently deepen your experience of God. Few spiritual disciplines offer so much benefit for so little effort.

Professing Our Faith

The prayer that we say while making the sign derives from Jesus' command, reported in Matthew 28:19, that the Church should baptize new disciples "in the name of the Father and of the Son and of the Holy Spirit." This formula evolved into longer creeds by which converts declared their faith at baptism. By the end of the fourth century, newly baptized Christians in the churches of the East professed the Nicene Creed, which we now recite at Sunday Mass. Converts in Western churches confessed the Apostles' Creed, which St. Ambrose (ca. 339–97) named in the fourth century and attributed to the Twelve. The text of that familiar prayer reads as follows:

I believe in God, the Father almighty,
     creator of heaven and earth.
I believe in Jesus Christ, his only Son, our Lord.
He was conceived by the power of the Holy Spirit
     and born of the Virgin Mary.
Under Pontius Pilate He
     was crucified, died, and was buried.
He descended to the dead.
On the third day he rose again.
He ascended into heaven
     and is seated at the right hand of the Father.
He will come again to judge the living
     and the dead.

I believe in the Holy Spirit,
     the holy catholic Church,
     the communion of saints,
     the forgiveness of sins,
     the resurrection of the body,
     and the life everlasting. Amen.[2]

Each time we make the sign of the cross we renew our profession of faith in these truths in an abbreviated but spiritually dense form. We express our belief in and commitment to the Father, Son, and Holy Spirit, and we acknowledge their work of creation, salvation, and sanctification.

In a practice rooted in the past, many Christians believe that even without our pronouncing the words "In the name of . . . ," the gesture itself confesses our faith. They hold that making the sign affirms essential Christian doctrines: touching our forehead and descending to our breast declares that we believe that the Father sent his Son from heaven to earth to assume our human nature; touching the left shoulder confesses that the Son died on the cross to bring us salvation; and moving to the right shoulder professes our faith in his ascension to heaven and his sending of the Holy Spirit to sanctify us.

Whether I sign myself silently or with the invocation, it helps me to look beyond the mundane things I have to do every day—family duties, work, study, car and yard maintenance, pet care, and so forth—and focus on God and on the greater part of reality, the part that is spiritual and invisible. Making the sign is an opportunity to profess

my faith in God and put him first in my thoughts, where
he belongs.

Addressing the God Who Is

Relying too heavily on our imagined ideas of God may
weaken or distort our relationship with him. Invoking
the Trinity when we sign ourselves helps us avoid this
unhappy condition.

Recently an interviewer on a national radio program
asked listeners what they did when they prayed. One
woman said she imagined God as being "very, very big"
and herself as "very, very small" as she stood before him.
Another person said he just "climbed up onto God's lap
and sat there with him." Using our imagination like this
can enhance our prayer, but it may also inhibit our coming to know God better and love him more.

In the worst-case scenario, too much imagining may
even cause us to worship our own idea of God instead of
God himself. For example, aided by artists' depictions,
some people conceive God the Father as a mighty old
man with a mane of white hair and a wildly flowing beard

framing a ferocious glance, garbed in rivers of silk, and traveling on a cloud.

In C. S. Lewis's classic *The Screwtape Letters*, the demon Screwtape, who is training his nephew Wormwood to seduce souls, advises the junior demon to encourage his "patient" to pray to the mental picture of God that he has constructed for himself. As you read the following passage, note that the demon refers to God as "the Enemy." The humans, says Screwtape,

> do not start from that direct perception of Him which we, unhappily, cannot avoid. . . . If you look into your patient's mind when he is praying, you will not find *that*. If you examine the object to which he is attending, you will find that it is a composite object containing many quite ridiculous ingredients. There will be images derived from pictures of the Enemy as He appeared during the discreditable episode known as the Incarnation; there will be vaguer—perhaps quite savage and puerile—images associated with the other two Persons. . . . But whatever the nature of the composite object, you must keep him praying to *it*—to the thing that

he has made, not to the Person who has made him.
. . . For if he ever comes to make the distinction, if
ever he consciously directs his prayers "Not to what
I think thou art but to what thou knowest thyself
to be," our situation is, for the moment, desperate.
Once all his thoughts and images have been flung
aside or, if retained, retained with a full recogni-
tion of their subjective nature, and the man trusts
himself to the completely real, external, invisible
Presence, there with him in the room and never
knowable by him as he is known by it—why, then
it is that the incalculable may occur.[3]

Here's where the sign of the cross comes in. When we
invoke the Trinity, we fix our attention on the God who
made us, not on the idea of God we have made. We fling
our images aside and address our prayers to God as he
has revealed himself to be: Father, Son, and Holy Spirit.
Sometimes after I have signed myself with the Trinitarian
formula, to be sure I'm getting it right I add "Lord, I am
praying to you as the God who knows who he is, not to
one who I think I know." In so fixing my gaze on the God
who is, I expect the incalculable to occur. I urge you to try

it. You will soon notice a difference in your prayer and in your disposition toward the Lord.

Coming into God's Presence

The word *name* has lost considerable weight since its usage in the Bible, where it conveyed a heavier meaning than it does now. If we are to experience the full benefit of praying "in the *name* of the Father, and of the Son, and of the Holy Spirit," we must recover the rich connotation that the name of God has in Scripture.

We regard a name as a label. It simply identifies the person who bears it. But for Jews in biblical times a name did much more. It related the person's nature and substance. Consider two examples, one from the Old Testament and one from the New Testament. When Jacob triumphed in his wrestling match with God, God gave him a new name that communicated his nature: "No longer are you to be called Jacob, but Israel since you have shown your strength against God and men and have prevailed" (Genesis 32:29). The name "Israel" means "He who strives with God." And in the New Testament, when Jesus met Simon he immediately gave him a new name that expressed his substance: "'So you are Simon the son of John? You shall be called Cephas' (which means Peter)" (John 1:42, RSV). The Aramaic "Cephas" and the Greek "Peter" both mean "rock."

Similarly, the name of God carries his nature and substance. When Moses asked God what his name was, he replied, "I am he who is." God also said to Moses, "This is what you are to say to the Israelites, 'I am has sent me to you'" (Exodus 3:14). Jesus told his divine name to Jewish leaders in a confrontation over his relationship to Abraham: "In all truth I tell you, before Abraham ever was, *I am*" (John 8:58; my emphasis). So God has revealed to us his name, a name that sums up his infinite existence and gives us access to him.

This biblical understanding of God's name opens us more fully to the spiritual power of the sign of the cross. When we make it while praying "in the name of" the Holy Trinity, we are praying in accord with God's divine nature and substance. We are praying in union with the God who is. Scripture teaches that when we call on his name, God draws near and blesses us. For example, when God made his covenant with Israel, he promised that "wherever I choose to have my name remembered, I shall come to you and bless you" (Exodus 20:24). Thus the invocation transports our prayer to a higher level by bringing us into the Lord's presence and engaging his power. So the sign of the cross is not merely a formula that opens and closes our prayers. It is a sacramental action that draws us near to God and makes us aware that we walk and pray in his company. Such a little gesture, so wonderful a consequence.

Praying with Godpower

Calling on God's name "supernaturalizes" our natural prayer. I like to say that by signing myself I am praying with Godpower instead of mere humanpower. And praying with Godpower makes a world of difference. By praying in God's name I am aligning my nature and substance with his nature and substance. This is what Jesus meant when he taught that if we asked anything in his name he would grant it. He repeated this promise five times in his farewell to the disciples the night before he died. He wanted to impress on us the tremendous advantage we have in appealing to his name. Jesus was also aware of our thick-headedness and used repetition to break through it. Just let his words sink into your mind and heart:

Whatever you ask in my name I will do,
so that the Father may be glorified in the Son.
If you ask me anything in my name,
I will do it (John 14:13–14).

The Father will give you
anything you ask him in my name (John 15:16).

In all truth I tell you,
anything you ask from the Father
he will grant in my name (John 16:23).

When that day comes
you will ask in my name;
and I do not say that I shall pray to the Father for
you,
because the Father himself loves you
for loving me,
and believing that I came from God
    (John 16:26–27).

Jesus does not mean that we can get whatever we want
by tacking the formula "in Jesus' name" onto our prayer

requests. Rather he taught us to align our wills with God's so that we will want what he wants and our prayer will become his prayer. That's the thrust of the prayer that the Lord gave us: "Our Father who art in heaven, / Hallowed be thy name. / Thy kingdom come. / Thy will be done, / On earth as it is in heaven" (Matthew 6:9–10, RSV). We reprise these words of the Lord's Prayer each time we sign ourselves.

The sign of the cross, then, with its lovely gesture and words, declares our decision to remain one with God and to embrace his will as our own. So praying *in the name of* the Blessed Trinity ensures that the Lord will answer our prayers because we are learning how to pray for what he holds foremost in his heart.

After I discovered the truths I have laid out in this chapter, I could not make the sign of the cross casually. I make it reverently and deliberately as an act of faith; as an appeal to the God who is, not the God I imagine him to be; and as a means of coming into his presence and aligning my will with his. I hope these truths touch you in the same way.

Now let's turn our attention to the sacrament of baptism and explore in detail its life-changing connection to the sign of the cross.

THREE

A Renewal of Baptism

Do you not know that all of us who have been baptized into Christ Jesus were baptized into his death? We were buried therefore with him by baptism into death, so that as Christ was raised from the dead by the glory of the Father, we too might walk in newness of life.

Romans 6:3–4, RSV

We come to the font as to the Red Sea. Moses was the leader in saving Israel; Christ was the leader in redeeming the human race. . . . The vast sea is divided by a rod; the entrance to the font is opened with the sign of the cross. Israel enters the sea; man is washed in the font.

St. Ildefonsus of Toledo (ca. 607–67)[1]

Let us not be ashamed of the Cross of Christ, but even if someone else conceals it, you must carry its mark publicly on your forehead, so that the demons, seeing the royal sign, trembling, may fly far away. Make this sign . . . on all occasions.

St. Cyril of Jerusalem[2]

E VERY YEAR ON A SUNDAY IN LENT millions of Catholics witness a striking reenactment of an ancient Christian ceremony. During Mass on that day, women and men who will be baptized at Easter are presented to the congregation. Their sponsors stand before them and claim them for Christ with the sign of the cross. The rite does not end once the sponsor has traced the little mark on his candidate's forehead. The sponsor then multiplies the sacred gesture, signing the candidate's eyes, ears, mouth, shoulders, hands, and feet. Finally, in a magnificent climax, he makes the sign of the cross over the person's entire body. This dramatic event thrills me each time I see it. I feel as though I have been transported back in time to a gathering in first-century Jerusalem and am watching the original Christian community prepare candidates for baptism.

As we have seen, receiving the mark of Christ at baptism taught the early Christians to make the sign of the cross (see page 20). And they kept in mind the connection between their baptismal signing and their signing themselves as a way of releasing the sacrament's power in their lives. St. Cyril of Jerusalem, for example, instructed new Christians both to bear confidently the baptismal mark in their persons and to sign themselves in all circumstances:

> Let us not be ashamed of the cross of Christ, but even if someone else conceals it, *you must carry its mark publicly on your forehead,* so that the demons, seeing the royal sign, trembling, may fly far away. *Make this sign* when you eat and when you drink, when you sit down, when you go to bed, when you get up, when you speak—in a word, on all occasions.[3]

We will do well to imitate our ancestors by making the same connection between our baptism and the sign of the cross—that is, that making the sign with faith activates the spiritual power of our baptism.

Three truths help us realize how signing ourselves awakens the spiritual energy that God gave us at baptism.

First, at our baptism we were buried with Christ and rose with him to a new, supernatural life. Second, Christ, by his cross, freed us from slavery to sin and death. Third, the Lord marked us with the sign of the cross as the seal of our participation in the new covenant and our incorporation into the Body of Christ. Think about these things with me and see how making the sign of the cross empowers us for daily Christian living.

A Sign of Supernatural Life

Immersion in water or pouring water on the head is the sacramental sign of baptism. The symbol speaks to us of water's cleansing power, and our first thought about it is that God uses it in baptism to wash away our sins. That's what the Church has always taught.[4] But the early Christians didn't perceive it that way. Their first thought about the symbol was not of water's power to cleanse but of its power to kill. For the Fathers of the Church, immersion in water at baptism was a death by drowning as well as a renewal in the Spirit—a participation in the death and rising of Christ.

St. Paul was the first to develop this teaching, and he expressed it most directly in his letter to the Romans. "Do you not know that all of us who have been baptized into Christ Jesus were baptized into his death? We were buried therefore with him by baptism into death, so that as Christ was raised from the dead by the glory of the Father, we too might walk in newness of life" (Romans 6:3–4, RSV). The Fathers elaborated on this theme, paralleling the actions of the sacrament to the events of the Crucifixion. St. Cyril of Jerusalem, for example, explained baptism to new Christians in this way:

> Then you were led to the holy pool of divine baptism, as Christ was carried from the cross to the tomb. . . . And each of you was asked whether he believed in the name of the Father, and of the Son, and of the Holy Spirit. You made that saving confession and you descended three times into the water and ascended, symbolizing the three days of Christ's burial. . . . For by this immersion and

rising you were both dying and being born. That
water of salvation was at once your grave and your
mother.[5]

We must bring this truth to bear on our understanding
of the way that baptism frees us of original sin. St. Paul
and the Fathers of the Church saw the consequence of
Adam's disobedience as the tragic loss of the supernatural
life that God had given him and planned to give to the
whole human race. At the tree of knowledge of good and
evil, Adam forfeited all the benefits of his intimate life
with God, especially the grace of seeing him face-to-face.
We must see original sin as our sharing in this great depri-
vation. But by his obedience at the tree of the cross, Jesus
recovered for us supernatural life with all of its benefits,
including the capacity to see God face-to-face, which will
be our reward in heaven. By our dying and rising with him
in our baptism, we receive the gift of that supernatural
life that Adam originally lost. "Just as all die in Adam,"
said St. Paul, "so in Christ all will be brought to life"
(1 Corinthians 15:22).

As God does in all the sacraments, he allows the sign
of baptism to accomplish what it signifies. He lets water

bring about our participation in Christ's death and rising. While making the sign of the cross reminds us of our baptism, the gesture does not possess in itself the power of a sacrament. But tracing the cross on our body and repeating the baptismal formula ("In the name of the Father . . .") expresses our faith and opens us to all the benefits of the new life Christ won for us.

A Sign of Our Spiritual Freedom

Early Christian writers regarded God's delivering Israel from slavery in Egypt at the Red Sea as a foreshadowing of his delivering us from slavery to sin and death at our baptism. They saw Moses' rod as a type of Christ's cross. "We come to the font as to the Red Sea," said Ildefonsus of Toledo, one of Spain's most loved saints:

> The Egyptians pursued the Israelites; sin pursued us. The sea is colored by the red of its shore; baptism is consecrated with the blood of Christ. The vast sea is divided by a rod; the entrance to the font is opened with the sign of the cross. Israel enters the

sea; we are washed in the font. . . . The pursuing
Egyptians are drowned with Pharaoh; sins are
destroyed in baptism together with the devil in a
destruction not of life but of power.[6]

We believe that baptism frees us from sin and death,
and making the sign of the cross can play a very practical
role in applying this truth to our lives. Signing ourselves
can help us experience our spiritual freedom.

In Romans 6, Paul suggests that it is not enough to realize that by our baptism we are dead to sin:

> We *know* that our old self was crucified with him
> so that the sinful body might be destroyed, and we
> might no longer be enslaved to sin. . . . So you also
> must *consider* yourselves dead to sin and alive to
> God in Christ Jesus.

> Let not sin therefore reign in your mortal bodies,
> to make you obey their passions. *Do not yield* your
> members to sin as instruments of wickedness,
> but *yield yourselves to God* as men who have been

brought from death to life, and your members to
God as instruments of righteousness (Romans 6:6,
11–13, RSV; my emphasis).

We may *know* that we have died to sin, but if we fail
to act on that knowledge, we may still give in to it. Paul
insists that we must hold ourselves to the truth—we must
"consider [ourselves] dead to sin and alive to God." That
means we must think about it, regard it, dwell on it, mull
over it, meditate on it, take it into account, and so on.

He also insists that we must refuse to yield to sin and
that we must decide to yield ourselves to God. That means
we must not give in, give way, surrender, or submit to sin
but must give in, give way, surrender, and submit to God.

That's what we do when we make the sign of the cross.
Signing ourselves is a way of considering ourselves dead to
sin and alive to God. It is a practical means for refusing
to yield to sin and for yielding ourselves to God. So when
temptation knocks, the best way to let it know that "no
one's home" is to make the sign of the cross. As St. Paul
says, "Someone who has died, of course, no longer has to
answer for sin" (Romans 6:7).

So at my morning prayer, especially on days when I feel tired and am more susceptible to irritability and other temptations, I sign myself, saying, "I died with Christ. I'm a dead man, and dead men cannot sin. Help me today, Lord, to tame my anger with patience." And during the day I frequently make little crosses on my forehead as a way of refusing temptation and yielding to God.

A Sign of Membership in the Church

Scripture draws a parallel between circumcision and baptism. St. Paul, for example, speaks about baptism in this way: "In [Christ] you have been circumcised, with a circumcision performed, not by human hand, but by the complete stripping of your natural self. This is circumcision according to Christ" (Colossians 2:11). Just as the rite of circumcision sealed the old covenant alliance between God and his people and incorporated them into Israel, baptism seals the new covenant alliance between God and us and incorporates us into the new Israel, the Church. And just as participation in the old covenant was conveyed by the mark of circumcision, our participation in the new covenant is conveyed by the mark of baptism—the sign of the cross.

At baptism the celebrant, our sponsor, and our parents (if we are baptized as an infant) seal our union with God and our membership in the Body of Christ by marking our body with the sign of the cross. At the same time, God seals these relationships by marking our spirit. Again speaking of baptism, St. Paul says, "You have been stamped with the seal of the Holy Spirit" (Ephesians 1:13). Once we are sealed by the Holy Spirit we have access to the spiritual benefits of the sacraments. Thus baptism is the doorway to our celebrating all of the other sacraments. When we trace the cross over our body we acknowledge what baptism has accomplished for us.

A Simple Sign That Activates Our Baptism

The early Christians traced the cross on their forehead to remind themselves that by their baptism they lived a supernatural life in the Body of Christ. The external mark expressed an inner grace, the presence of God himself. It works the same for us today. Each time we trace the cross over our body, we ask the Lord to refresh the life in the

Holy Spirit that we received in baptism. I recommend that you do this deliberately. Sign yourself, and as you pray the words that consecrated you to the Lord in baptism, ask him to strengthen your union with him and to energize you with a new outpouring of the Holy Spirit. Can you think of an easier way to bring the grace of the sacrament into your life? Can you imagine any simpler way to fully employ the spiritual power that the Lord has placed at your disposal? I can't. As we make the sign of the cross, the Lord pours into us a stream of baptismal grace—the Holy Spirit, whom he described as a river of living water that would flow from the hearts of those who believed in him (see John 7:37–38).

A simple gesture that we perform before Mass sums up the truths of this chapter. Each time we enter church we dip our fingers into holy water and make the sign of the cross. We must recognize the significance of that action, for by it we are reminding ourselves that we have been baptized and that the cross seals our membership in the Body of Christ. By signing ourselves we display the credentials that authorize us to participate in the Holy Eucharist, the highest of the sacraments, and to join the Lord in offering his perfect sacrifice.

Jesus designed baptism as a source of new life for those he called to become his disciples, and in the next chapter we will consider the connection between the sign of the cross and following him. You will notice that from this point on the going gets tougher. Making the sign calls for follow-through actions that require hard decisions. Its demands are difficult, but the spiritual rewards it offers are great.

FOUR

A Mark of Discipleship

Then he said to them all: "If anyone would come after me, he must deny himself and take up his cross daily and follow me."

Luke 9:23, NIV

~

As soon as the Redeemer had restored us to our liberty he marked us with his sign, the sign of the cross. So we bear on our forehead the same sign that is engraved on the doors of palaces. The Conqueror places it there so that all may know that he has reentered into possession of us, and that we are his palaces, his living temples.

St. Caesarius of Arles[1]

~

Thanks be to you, my Lord Jesus Christ, for all the benefits you have given me, for all the pains and insults you have borne for me. O most merciful redeemer, friend and brother, may I know you more clearly, love you more dearly and follow you more nearly, day by day.

St. Richard of Wyche, bishop of Chichester (ca. 1197–1253)[2]

WHEN I MAKE the sign of the cross I am declaring publicly that I am a Christian. I am saying to all that I am a follower of Christ. That's a serious matter, given what he requires of all his disciples. "If anyone would come after me," he said, "he must deny himself and take up his cross daily and follow me. For whoever wants to save his life will lose it, but whoever loses his life for me will save it" (Luke 9:23–24, NIV).

If we think we are following a meek and mild Jesus who will make things easy for us, we had better think again. As his challenging words indicate, the Lord is both good and tough, loving and demanding. We follow him at a great cost, but he rewards us with greater benefits. Evangelical missionary Oswald Chambers (1874–1917) said that the Lord calls us to give our "utmost for his highest." That's what we are promising when we sign ourselves.

I have a longtime friend who chose to follow Christ as a young man. Over the past quarter century he has often signed himself reverently as a way of renewing his decision. As he touches his forehead, he prays, "Father, love me." He moves his hand to his breast, praying, "Son, live within me." Touching his shoulders, he prays, "Spirit, empower me." With a small gesture and a few words he keeps his commitment alive.

Signaling Our Self-Denial

Jesus said that his followers must deny themselves. We usually understand this obligation to mean that the Lord requires us to undertake the kind of fasting that we practice during Lent. In that season we abstain from eating meat, give up candy or desserts, skip meals, and so on. Jesus surely had such fasting in mind when he called us to deny ourselves. He predicted that his followers would fast when he was gone and prescribed that we do our fasting secretly (see Matthew 6:16–18; 9:15). He taught us to renounce our selfish attachments to the good things of earth as a way to anticipate the better things of heaven.

But when Jesus said that his followers must deny themselves, he also meant something else, something deeper. He
was establishing the terms on which he, the master, would
relate to us, his disciples. As the condition of accepting
us as followers, Jesus requires us to surrender control of
our lives to him. Here Jesus, our Lord and teacher, is
following the practice of rabbis of his day, who demanded
the total submission of their pupils. This is the true
meaning of self-denial: Jesus expects us to *deny* that we
belong to ourselves and to *declare* that we belong to him.

When we make that declaration, Jesus marks us as his
own. Neal Lozano illustrates this in his book *Unbound,*
where he tells about a young prodigal who turned to
Christ by signing himself morning and night before reading the Gospel of John, saying "Come and get me, Jesus!"
After two months, Jesus took up the young man's offer,
reclaimed him as a disciple, and restored him to an active
Christian life.[3]

The Fathers of the Church taught that this shift in ownership occurred at our baptism when the celebrant marked
us with the sign of the cross. They used the Greek word
sphragis (sfrag-ece), a term that was pregnant with meaning

about discipleship, to name both the baptismal seal and the sign of the cross.

In the ancient world a *sphragis* was a sign of ownership that a person placed on his possessions. For example, a shepherd marked his sheep as his property with a brand that he called a *sphragis*, and a Roman general claimed new recruits by tattooing a *sphragis*—usually an abbreviated form of the general's name—on their forearms. The *sphragis* was not only a declaration of ownership. It also brought benefits to those whom it marked. A shepherd protected and provided for those sheep that carried his brand. The general pledged loyalty and support to the soldiers who wore his sign.

The Fathers of the Church borrowed from the ancient practices of branding sheep and tattooing soldiers to explain how Christ claimed us as his own at our baptism. They taught that Christ used the sign of the cross to incorporate new believers into his flock. For instance, St. Cyril of Jerusalem, addressing candidates for baptism, invited them to "come, receive the sacramental seal so that you may be easily recognized by the Master. Be numbered among the holy and spiritual flock of Christ, so that you may be set at his right hand and inherit the life prepared for you."[4]

The Fathers also taught that just as the shepherd's brand protected his sheep from danger, the sign of the cross defends us from our spiritual enemies. "If you fortify yourself with the *sphragis*," said St. Gregory Nazianzen (ca. 329–90), "and secure yourself for the future with the best and strongest of all aids, being signed both in body and in soul with the anointing, . . . what then can happen to you and what has been worked out for you? . . . This, even while you live, will greatly contribute to your sense of safety. For a sheep that is sealed is not easily snared, but that which is unmarked is an easy prey to thieves."[5]

For the Fathers, the general's marking of his soldiers with his name was even more helpful in explaining how Christ took possession of us with the sign of the cross. When recruits enlisted in the Roman army, they participated in a religious ceremony, during which they took a loyalty oath called a *sacramentum*. Then a general marked them as belonging to him with his *sphragis*. The Fathers saw a parallel between this practice and baptism. During a formal ceremony at the beginning of Lent, new believers in the early Church would enroll for baptism at Easter. At the Easter Vigil, the candidates would take their loyalty oath to Christ by professing faith in him. (The Fathers had in mind this Christian *sacramentum* when they invented the name for the Catholic sacraments.) Then, through the agency of the celebrant, Christ would mark their body and soul as belonging to him with his *sphragis,* the sign of the cross, which is the baptismal seal. St. Cyril put these words in the Lord's mouth: "After my battle on the cross, I gave to each of my soldiers the right to wear on their forehead the royal *sphragis.*"[6]

So the sign of the cross says a lot about my relationship with the Lord. Tracing it on my body declares that as his disciple, I no longer belong to myself, but I belong to him. It signifies that he has incorporated me into his flock, having placed in my person the mark of his ownership. The sign I wear proudly on my forehead announces that I have enlisted as a soldier in his army and that I count on him for his loyalty and protection.

Acknowledging the Lord's Ownership

It would be nice if we behaved as though we really believed that the Lord owned us. But we don't. We easily forget that we have entrusted ourselves to him and we conduct ourselves as though everything really belonged to us.

We must overcome the conditioning that trains us to believe that we own everything. We learn to say the words "my" and "mine" as toddlers and then we apply them universally, from "my blanket" and "my puppy" to "my body," "my time," "my life," and even "my God."

We may forgive a toddler for believing that he owns the blanket that his mother knit for him and the terrier that his father bought him. But we should rid ourselves of the notion that we own the body, time, and life that God has given us. We arrive in a body and leave it both at moments God chooses without our consent. We have no control over time or life, which are God's constant gifts to us. And we make a horrific mistake if we reverse the true order of reality and dare to act as though the expression "my God" means something like "my puppy" instead of "the God I worship."

The sign of the cross helps us there. Making it frequently reminds us to recognize that we are the Lord's possession. It prompts us to behave accordingly. I sometimes sign myself while saying, "Lord, I acknowledge that you own me and everything about me." Then I sign myself again, saying, "Lord, I know that my body, my time, and my life really belong to you, not to me." And I sign myself a third time, saying, "Lord, you are my God, the God I worship with everything I have and am." I recommend this practice. I encourage you to make the sign of the cross while acknowledging in your own words that the Lord owns your body, time, and life—that he owns you.

Making this shift in ownership may at first strike you as burdensome and painful. None of us feels good about surrendering control over our most intimate possessions. But you will soon discover that acknowledging Christ's ownership and entrusting yourself to him alleviates your worry and allows you to receive his care. Jesus promised just that when he said, "Shoulder my yoke and learn from me, for I am gentle and humble in heart, and you will find rest for your souls. Yes, my yoke is easy and my burden light" (Matthew 11:29–30).

Following Jesus

Self-denial is the Lord's first condition for would-be disciples. He requires two things further: disciples must take up their cross daily, and then they must follow him. We will consider the subject of bearing our cross in the next chapter. Here we will talk about the role that the sign of the cross plays in our following Jesus.

Disciples follow Jesus by embracing his teaching and obeying his commandments. Making the sign of the cross says that we accept these requirements of our discipleship. That's a big commitment, and to keep it we must understand all that it involves.

Embracing Christ's teaching. This little book's limited scope prevents me from summarizing the Lord's teaching, but I can point readers to the best resources for learning about it. We find Christ's teaching in the Bible, in the doctrine of the Church, and in books of theology. The place to start is the Gospels, especially Jesus' longer discourses: the Sermon on the Mount (Matthew 5–7) and his farewell address (John 13:31–17:26). Then you will want to explore his instruction in the other New Testament books and study the rest of God's teaching in the Old Testament.

The Lord made the Church the custodian of his teaching, and you will discover the heart of it in the *Catechism of the Catholic Church* and in the documents of Vatican Council II.[7] Among many excellent popular theology books that recap Christ's doctrine and reflect on it, I recommend my two favorites: *Theology and Sanity* by F. J. Sheed and *The Catholic Vision* by Edward D. O'Connor, C.S.C.[8]

We study Christ's teaching not to get better informed but to receive the truth and apply it to our lives. So as we read Scripture, the *Catechism,* and theology books, we must ask questions such as "What is the Lord saying to me here?" "What does this mean for me?" and "What must I do about it?" It's just good common sense to begin our study by making the sign of the cross. In this way we approach the Lord's teaching by calling on his name.

Signing ourselves in the name of the Father, and of the Son, and of the Holy Spirit declares our desire to know the truth that God has revealed about creation, redemption, and the spiritual life. Without these divinely inspired perspectives, said F. J. Sheed, we are doomed to a narrow-minded, insane view of things.[9] If we do not apprehend the truths the Lord has revealed—most of which are spiritual, invisible, and inaccessible to the senses—we are technically mad, because we are out of touch with the greater part of reality. So I advise disciples to make the sign of the cross as an appeal to the Lord for his wisdom and for the mental and spiritual health that comes from seeing things with his eyes.

Obeying Christ's commandments. When we read the Gospels we learn that Jesus not only affirmed the Ten Commandments but also raised them to an even higher standard of holiness. "Do not imagine," he said, "that I have come to abolish the Law or the Prophets. I have come not to abolish but to complete them" (Matthew 5:17). He taught us that two great commandments sum up the Ten: "Love the Lord your God with all your heart and with all your soul and with all your mind" and "Love your neighbor as yourself" (Matthew 22:37, 39, NIV). He also gave us numerous specific commands, such as "Love your enemies" (Matthew 5:44), "Do not store up treasures for yourselves on earth" (Matthew 6:19), and "Do not judge" (Matthew 7:1).

We must not skip over any of these, but as good disciples we must determine how well we are obeying each of them. I find it helpful to ask myself the following question: What one thing can I do to obey more fully this command of Christ? When we are trying to figure out how fully to respond to a commandment, signing ourselves can help because it reminds us that Christ's own obedience took him to the cross. It signals our willingness to crucify our comfort, our preferences, our stubbornness, and anything that stands in the way of our obeying him.

Just before he died Jesus gave us a commandment that subsumes all the others: "Love one another, as I have loved you. No one can have greater love than to lay down his life for his friends" (John 15:12–13). St. John explained that obeying Jesus' command to love others as he did was the supreme way to obey the command to love God above all. "Whoever does not love does not know God, because God is love. . . . [I]f we love one another, God lives in us and his love is made complete in us. . . . [A]nyone who does not love his brother, whom he has seen, cannot love God, whom he has not seen" (1 John 4:8, 12, 20, NIV). I believe that making the sign of the cross expresses our decision to obey this, the highest of Jesus' commandments. I trace the trunk of the cross from my forehead to my breast to pledge my love for God and the bar across my shoulders to pledge my love for others. The act says that I lay down my life for others as a sign of my love for God.

Now we will turn our attention to Jesus' requirement that disciples take up their cross daily. We will see how making the sign of the cross is an acceptance of suffering, the ultimate act of love for God and others.

FIVE

An Acceptance
of Suffering

In the world you will have hardship,
but be courageous:
I have conquered the world.

John 16:33

Be merciful to me, O God, be merciful to me,
   for in you my soul takes refuge;
in the shadow of your wings I will take refuge,
   until the destroying storms pass by.

Psalm 57:1, NRSV

In [Christ's] suffering he stretched forth his hands and measured
out the world, that even then he might show that a great multitude,
collected together out of all languages and tribes, from the rising of
the sun even to its setting, was about to come under his wings, and
to receive on their foreheads that great and lofty sign.

Lactantius (ca. 250–ca. 325)[1]

W E ARE TEMPTED TO BELIEVE that just by being good Christians we can make suffering go away. We imagine that God's promise of blessing means that he will spare us all pain. But it doesn't work that way. Jesus made suffering a normal part of the Christian life. He promised his disciples multiple blessings, but tacked onto the end of the good things he said they could expect was a promise of suffering: "There is no one who has left house, brothers, sisters, mother, father, children or land for my sake and for the sake of the gospel who will not receive a hundred times as much, houses, brothers, sisters, mothers, children and land—and persecutions too—now in this present time and, in the world to come, eternal life" (Mark 10:29–30). So suffering is not an option for Christians. It's a guarantee.

At root, the word *suffering* means enduring pain or distress, sustaining loss or damage, being subject to disability or sickness, and ultimately submitting to death. It comes in all shapes. Daily nuisances frustrate us. Repeated failures discourage us. Bills we cannot pay pressure us. A disintegrating relationship racks us. Depression defeats us. Violence wounds us or harms a loved one. Illness ravages us or overtakes a family member. Suffering afflicts everybody.

Jesus not only promised suffering; he also made bearing personal crosses a daily requirement for all of his followers (see Luke 9:23, NIV). Making the sign of the cross proclaims our yes to this condition of discipleship. When we sign ourselves we are taking up our cross and accepting whatever suffering comes our way. With that ancient gesture we are saying that we welcome suffering on God's terms. And we are subordinating our will—that would rather not endure pain—to God, just as Jesus subordinated his will to his Father when he gave himself to the cross. So tracing Christ's cross over our body has serious consequences.

Safety in the Shadow of His Wings

Christians attempt to comfort sufferers by touting the benefits of suffering. "Suffering builds character," we say.

"I don't want character," says the sufferer. "I want relief." Then come the inevitable questions: "Why does God let bad things happen?" and "Where is God when it hurts?"

The care that parents give their children suggests answers to both questions. For example, suppose a seven-year-old girl is taking her first ride on a bicycle. Her father, running alongside her, sees that she is about to hit a rough spot on the road but restrains his impulse to reach out and steady the bike. The dad wants his little girl to learn how to ride with confidence, so he does not prevent her fall. When the bike bounces off the bump, the girl panics, tumbles to the pavement, and scrapes her elbow and knee. The dad scoops her up into his arms and comforts her. Then he carries her into the house, cleans and dresses her scratches, holds her on his lap, and tells her a favorite story.

God is like that dad. He lets us navigate our way, but he stays alongside us. He does not prevent bad things from happening because he wants us to learn to deal confidently with hardship. But when we suffer, God scoops us up and stays with us. He shares our pain, sustains us, and consoles us.

That's the message of the cross, and signing ourselves opens us to hearing it. God's only Son became a man in Christ. In his human nature, God himself suffered rejection, humiliation, ridicule, abandonment, buffetings, scourging, crucifixion, and death. He embraced suffering as a man so that he could comfort us in our suffering.

When we make the sign of the cross we invite the Lord to join us in our suffering. We touch our forehead and move down to our breast, telling the Lord with this gesture that we want him to bend down to us. Then we cross our shoulders in a movement that asks him to support us—to shoulder us—in our suffering. In many psalms, David sings of taking refuge beneath the Lord's wings, which the Church Fathers understood as a prophecy of our finding safety in the shadow of his crucified arms (see Psalms 17:8; 36:7; 57:1; 61:4; 63:7). The Lord's outstretched arms pledge that he understands our suffering and shares it with us.

Just as the psalms anticipate the grace of Christ's crucifixion, the Old Testament book of Deuteronomy provided another foreshadowing of the cross as a place of refuge. It reported Moses' farewell address, in which he seemed to describe the silhouette of the cross in the far distance. He assured Israel that the arms of the Lord would uphold them through all their troubles: "The eternal God is your dwelling place, and underneath are the everlasting arms" (Deuteronomy 33:27, RSV).

Today we see the cross clearly as a sign of God's mercy and consolation. I take advantage of the grace and support the Lord offers me with his outstretched arms. When trouble strikes, I sign myself often, saying, "Lord, scoop me up in your everlasting arms, carry me through this trial, and comfort me." Strengthened by his response to that simple gesture and prayer, I find the hardship endurable.

Sharing in Christ's Suffering for the Church

In signing ourselves, we not only ask Jesus to share in our suffering, but we also declare our willingness to participate in his. As St. Paul tells us, "You have been granted the privilege for Christ's sake not only of believing in him but of suffering for him as well; you are fighting the same battle which you saw me fighting for him and which you hear I am fighting still" (Philippians 1:29–30). Peter says we should be glad about this, because entering into the Lord's suffering now will bring us a great reward in the future (see 1 Peter 4:12–13).

We face adversities every day because we are engaged with Christ in his spiritual combat for the Church. We easily lose sight of this reality and view our troubles and tragedies as inconveniences, bad luck, calamitous accidents, or "just the way things are." But from the beginning Jesus conscripted his followers to join him in waging war against enemy forces, the evil spirits who resisted his effort to bring men and women into his kingdom. And this activity results in an experience of suffering on our part, as we are fighting a powerful foe.

Our patient endurance of hardship in itself can contribute to Christ's work for the Church. It can become a prayer that touches the lives of others. Elizabeth Leseur (1866–1914), a French woman who suffered from cancer for many years and is currently a candidate for canonization, taught that our suffering can become an opportunity of grace for others:

> I know by experience that in hours of trial certain graces are obtained for others that all our efforts had not previously obtained. I have thus concluded that suffering is the higher form of action, the best expression in the wonderful communion of saints. . . .

Through it God consents to accomplish everything.
Suffering helps Christ to save the world and souls.
When I am overwhelmed by the immensity of my
desires for those I love, . . . it is toward suffering that
I turn. It is through suffering that I ask to be allowed
to serve as an intermediary between God and souls.
It is the perfect form of prayer, the only infallible
form of action. . . . Through the cross to the Light.[2]

After Elizabeth's death in 1914, her husband, Felix, an
atheist, read her journals. He discovered there that she
had offered years of great suffering for him. Felix was so
moved that he not only embraced Christ but also became
a Dominican priest and traveled throughout Europe
speaking about his wife's spiritual writings.

A right and healthy perspective on suffering comes
down to this: Christ won the war for our salvation on the
cross, but he has called us to apply his victory in our daily
lives. He has enlisted us as collaborators in his effort to
draw people into his Church and defend it, and our col-
laboration with him opens us to suffering. "Trouble," said
St. Ambrose, "comes only to those on their way to glory."[3]
Making the sign of the cross over our body is a way of

saying yes to the battle and of accepting hardship as our share of Christ's suffering.

We have touched on the war being waged between Christ's army and the enemy forces. Now we will consider directly our role in the Lord's spiritual warfare and how the sign of the cross is our defense against the devil.

SIX

A Defense against the Devil

This was the purpose of the appearing of the Son of God, to undo the work of the devil.

1 John 3:8

∼

It is the sign of the faithful and the dread of devils, for on the cross he triumphed over them and openly paraded their defeat. So when they see the cross, they remember the Crucified. They fear him who crushed the heads of the demons.

St. Cyril of Jerusalem[1]

∼

The sign of the cross is the type of our deliverance. . . . When you make it, remember what has been given for your ransom, and you will be the slave of no one. Make it, then, not only with your fingers, but with your faith. So if you engrave it on your forehead, no impure spirit will dare to stand before you. He sees the blade by which he has been wounded, the sword by which he has received his death blow.

St. John Chrysostom[2]

W HEN I GIVE A TALK about the saints, invariably someone asks me why the Church demoted St. Christopher. I explain that the Church did not demote St. Christopher but removed his feast day from the calendar of the saints because we have so very little information about him. We know only that he died as a martyr during a persecution in the mid–third century.

Today we revere and invoke St. Christopher as the patron of travelers, but we would do better to remember him for the reason he became a most popular saint in the Middle Ages. In those centuries, Christians celebrated him not because he guaranteed safety on the road or at sea but because his legend demonstrated the power of the sign of the cross over the devil. Christopher's story goes something like this:

Christopher, a magnificent giant, left home in search of the most powerful king in the world so that he could serve him. On his travels he first met a great Christian king and pledged to follow him. One day a jester entertained the royal court with a song about the devil, and every time the king heard the word "devil" he made the sign of the cross. Puzzled by this strange gesture, Christopher asked the king what it meant. "Whenever I hear the devil mentioned," said the king, "I defend myself with this sign for fear that he might get some power over me and do me harm."

"If you are afraid of the devil," said Christopher, "he must be stronger and greater than you. So goodbye! I am going to look for the devil and enter his service because he must be the most powerful king on earth."

A short time later, as Christopher was walking along a road, he met a large army. Their leader, a formidable-looking warrior, asked him where he was going. Christopher said, "I'm searching for the devil. I want to take him as my master."

"I'm the one you're looking for," said the warrior. Glad to have found the devil, Christopher promised to serve him and joined his army. As the army continued their march, they passed a roadside cross. When the devil noticed it, he was terrified and hid behind a boulder. Shocked by his new master's behavior, Christopher asked him what made him so afraid. The devil hemmed and hawed, refusing to answer, but Christopher insisted. So the devil relented and said, "Once a man named Jesus Christ was nailed to a cross, and when I see his sign, it fills me with terror, and I run from it."

"If that's the case," said Christopher, "then this Jesus is greater and more powerful than you. Therefore, I still haven't found the greatest king on earth. So I'm leaving you. I'm going to search for Christ and make him my master."

Later in the story, Christopher finds Christ while he is working as a ferryman, carrying people across a river. He takes Christ as his king and serves him even in martyrdom.[3]

The Devil's Defeat

Today, centuries after St. Christopher's time, the sign of the cross still maintains its power over Satan. He continues to cower and turn tail at the sight of it. So making the sign still protects us from our most dangerous enemy, but here's the funny thing: even though the sign of the cross ensures our victory in our battles with the devil, we don't use it very much. It is a mighty, surefire weapon right at hand, but we ignore it.

Why don't we take advantage of this powerful weapon? I think the reason has to do with our attitude toward the devil. Many people just don't have him on their radar screen. They believe the devil exists, but with their eyes fixed on everyday things they don't pay him any attention. Others, fewer in number, don't believe the devil exists and so don't see that an enemy lurks about waiting to snare them. Neither of these two groups uses the sign as an instrument of spiritual warfare because they do not realize that they are at war.

But we are embroiled in a war with the devil, and the stakes are high because our salvation is at risk. The devil's very name signals our great danger. The word *devil* derives from the Greek *diabolos*, which at root means "throw across." Indeed, the devil throws himself across God's plan to rescue us from sin and death, attempting to block it.

Jesus himself spoke clearly about Satan's threat to humankind. He said that the devil was "a murderer from the start" and "a liar, and the father of lies" (John 8:44). He declared that his purpose in life was to redeem all humanity from Satan's grip by submitting to death on the cross. He said, "Now the prince of this world is to be driven out. And when I am lifted up from the earth, I shall draw all people to myself" (John 12:31–32).

Christ's victory on the cross came as a complete surprise to the devil. He had expected that he would win by taking the life of God's Son. Satan did have a claim against human beings. He knew that because of our sins we had a debt to pay that would cost us our lives. But he made a huge mistake by attempting to take the life of Christ, the sinless one against whom he had no claim at all. Instead of the cross achieving the devil's great design to destroy Jesus, the cross cost him his control over all humanity.

The Fathers of the Church taught that had Satan realized what God intended to accomplish for us in Christ, he would never have pursued the Crucifixion. For instance, read carefully this reflection by St. Leo the Great (d. 461), who was pope in the mid–fifth century:

> That God might deliver humanity from the bonds
> of the death-bringing transgression, he concealed
> the power of Christ's majesty from the fury of
> the devil [see 1 Corinthians 2:8], and offered him
> instead the infirmity of our lowliness. For had this

proud and cruel enemy known the plan of God's mercy, he would have striven rather to temper with mildness the hearts of [those who crucified Christ] rather than to inflame them with evil hate, so that he might not lose the slavery of all his captives, while he pursued the liberty of the one who owed him nothing.

And so his own wickedness tricked him. He inflicted a torment on the Son of God that was changed into a medicine for all of the sons of men. He shed innocent blood, which became both the price and the drink that restored the world. The Lord . . . suffered upon himself the wicked hands of those who raged against him, who while intent on their crime yet served the plan of the Redeemer.[4]

So on that day nearly two thousand years ago the cross became Satan's ruin, and from that time its sign has paralyzed him with fear.

Applying Christ's Victory

Christ handed on to us the victory of his cross at our baptism (see chapter 3). The sacrament included one or more exorcisms in which the celebrant signed us with the cross while commanding the devil to depart from us. He also asked us to renounce Satan, which we did ourselves if we were baptized as adults or which our parents and godparents did in our name if we were baptized as infants.

As we have seen, God then used the waters of baptism to immerse us in the mystery of the cross itself. In the sacramental bath we died with Christ and then rose with him to a new life. At that pivotal moment the Lord marked us with the sign of the cross, the seal that claimed us as his. The Fathers of the Church taught that God stamped us with the sign of the cross to make us inviolable. With it he guaranteed our safety by warning the enemy not to harm or even touch us. Regarding baptism, St. Cyril of Jerusalem said, "The invocation of grace marking your soul with its seal prevents the terrible demon from swallowing you up."[5]

Our baptismal seal of inviolability equips us for victory in our daily battles with the devil. We engage its defensive and offensive properties each time we sign ourselves. The sign of the cross reminds the devil that we are Christ's possession and that he dare not injure us. The gesture repels him because it recalls the painful memory of his defeat.

Now here's a puzzle that may be bothering you, but it's only an apparent problem. If Christ conquered Satan on the cross, why is he still a threat to us? Why, for example, does St. Peter warn us that our "enemy the devil is on the prowl like a roaring lion, looking for someone to devour" (1 Peter 5:8)? If Jesus defeated him, why is he still free to roam around and cause us trouble?

An illustration from World War II casts some light on our situation with Satan. Although the war did not end until the summer of 1945, the victory of the Allies in Europe was assured in 1943. In that year factories in the United States began to produce more planes and ships than the Axis powers were destroying. Final victory was only a matter of time. The rest of the European campaign was one big mop-up operation.

Similarly, Christ won the war with Satan on the cross, but Satan has not yet left the field. Christ wanted to give us a piece of the action, so he recruited us to perform the mop-up operation. We, the members of the Church, the Body of Christ, have the privilege of enforcing the Lord's triumph over the devil. The tables are turned, and the intended victims of Satan's onslaught have become his conquerors.

So until Jesus comes again, we will have to fight skirmishes with the devil. No doubt about it, he is a dangerous adversary. But we must never forget that the Lord has given us the upper hand: he has won the war, and all we have to do is apply his victory in our daily lives. Like St. Christopher, we must take the Lord as our master and, armed with his holy sign, join him in battle against our mutual enemy.

In the next chapter we will learn how to employ the sign of the cross to defeat another enemy, one that we find within.

SEVEN

A Victory over Self-Indulgence

All who belong to Christ Jesus have crucified self with all its passions and its desires.

Since we are living by the Spirit, let our behaviour be guided by the Spirit and let us not be conceited or provocative and envious of one another.

Galatians 5:24–26

∽

We must expect the cure of all our wounds from the sign of the cross. If the venom of avarice courses through our veins, let's make the sign of the cross, and the venom will be expelled. . . . If the basest of worldly thoughts seek to defile us, let's again make the sign of the cross, and we shall live the divine life.

St. Maximus of Turin (ca. 380–ca. 467)[1]

∽

You have stripped off your old behaviour with your old self, and you have put on a new self which will progress toward true knowledge the more it is renewed in the image of its Creator.

Colossians 3:9–10

I HAVE HAD LIFELONG PROBLEMS with anger, impatience, and criticalness, to name a few of my troublesome flaws. When I find myself trapped in wrongdoing arranged by one of them, my occasional first instinct is to blame someone else. Sometimes, for example, I imagine that I caught my anger, like a virus, from my feisty Italian-American mother. Think about your problems. Do you struggle with anger, as I do? Or do you have a problem with jealousy, or lust, or laziness, or addiction, or some other bad behavior? Like me, do you sometimes blame your problem on someone else, perhaps your mom or dad?

Such excuses contain a germ of truth. Family patterns influence our conduct. But the real origin of unruly behavior is within us, in our heart. That's where Jesus located the source of our sinful problems. "From the heart," he said, "come evil intentions: murder, adultery, fornication, theft, perjury, slander" (Matthew 15:19). To this list he could well have added, among many others, the famous seven capital sins, those deadly vices that we struggle with: arrogance, rage, envy, sloth, gluttony, greed, and lust.

Scripture calls this root cause of our problems "the flesh" or "self-indulgence." For example, St. Paul says, "The works of the flesh are plain: fornication, impurity, licentiousness, idolatry, sorcery, enmity, strife, jealousy, anger, selfishness, dissension, party spirit, envy, drunkenness, carousing, and the like" (Galatians 5:19–21, RSV). I prefer the term *self-indulgence* because to the sex-saturated contemporary mind the word *flesh* suggests that the body or sexuality instigates our problems, which is not what Scripture is saying. Rather the Bible points to a force within that seduces us to sin.

We cozy up to our self-indulgence because it licenses bad things that we like to do. We also pretend that because of its influence we cannot stop committing our favorite sins. I used to think that I just could not prevent myself from occasionally exploding with rage. I have learned that this was a convenient lie that permitted me to hang on to my pet wrongdoing. The truth is that the Lord confers on us in baptism the power to deal effectively with our self-indulgence. In that sacrament he frees us by the power of his cross so that we no longer have to obey the siren song of sin. In baptism he also gives us the sign of the cross as a means of curbing our evil tendencies. I think you will agree that it is a very practical tool.

Crucifying Our Base Desires

We can deal with problems that stem from our evil tendencies in one of two ways. We can either give in to them or fight them. Neither way is easy because both hurt. Giving in to bad behaviors causes pain for us and for the people we love. And fighting sinful problems hurts because it requires us to kill our self-indulgence.

So when we decide that we want to get free of a problem, we have a fight on our hands. We are siding with the Spirit we received in baptism in its war against self-indulgence. "The desires of self-indulgence," said St. Paul, "are always in opposition to the Spirit, and the desires of the Spirit are in opposition to self-indulgence" (Galatians 5:17). Our strategy in this spiritual warfare is to kill self-indulgence by saying no to the evil behaviors that it promotes. St. Paul said, "You must kill everything in you that is earthly: sexual vice, impurity, uncontrolled passion, evil desires and especially greed. . . . [Y]ou also must give up all these things: human anger, hot temper, malice, abusive language and dirty talk" (Colossians 3:5, 8).

When we engage in this battle against self-indulgence we can expect to go at it for a long time. We do not have a silver bullet that will put it to death instantly. Scripture says that we must crucify our self-indulgence, and crucifixion is a slow, agonizing form of death: "All who belong to Christ Jesus," said St. Paul, "have crucified self with all its passions and its desires" (Galatians 5:24).

We can employ the sign of the cross as a most appropriate instrument for this purpose. While making the gesture every morning we can say something like "Lord, today by the power of your cross I refuse to give in to my problem with envy" (or whatever behavior that bedevils you). If you were a fly on the wall in my living room during my prayer time, you might witness me signing myself and saying, "Lord, I put my anger to death on this cross. Give me the strength to say no to it today."

The *today* is a very important part of such prayers. We can readily resist our self-indulgence one day at a time, but if we were to declare that we would never again yield to anger, envy, or any other evil impulse, we might soon find ourselves defeated and discouraged. The *never* in such a statement foolishly creates an opportunity for self-indulgence to ambush us. Having pledged to never succumb to these tendencies, we would imagine we were safe and would soon lower our defenses. Never is a very long time, but today is manageable. Daily vigilance empowered by the cross ensures our ultimate victory.

So first thing in the morning we can refuse our evil tendencies with the sign of the cross. Then during the day we can sign ourselves to combat self-indulgence when it lures us to our favorite wrongdoing. The great Christian writers have always maintained confidence in the power of the sign to neutralize such temptations. "Who is the man," asked St. Bernard of Clairvaux (1090–1153), "so completely master of his thoughts as never to have impure ones? But it is necessary to repress their attacks immediately so that we may vanquish the enemy where he hoped to triumph. The infallible means of success is to make the sign of the cross."[2] And Origen (ca. 185–ca. 254), a third-century theologian, summed up the role of the sign of the cross in our overcoming self-indulgence: "Such is the power of the sign of the cross that if we place it before our eyes, if we keep it faithfully in our heart, neither concupiscence, nor sensuality, nor anger can resist it. At its appearance the whole army of self-indulgence and sin take to flight."[3]

Clothing Ourselves with Christ

Our victory over self-indulgence is not merely a matter of eliminating our bad behaviors. We must learn to replace our anger, meanness, lustfulness, and other evil impulses with their opposites. And just as the sign of the cross helps us conquer our evil desires, it can also aid us in acquiring virtuous character traits like patience, kindness, and self-control.

As we have seen, our baptism was a radical, life-changing event. In it, by the power of his cross, Christ freed us from sin and death and gave us a new, supernatural life. We shed our old, sinful nature at the baptismal font and put on a new nature that was fashioned in the Lord's own image. "You have stripped off your old behaviour with your old self," said St. Paul, "and you have put on a new self which will progress towards true knowledge the more it is renewed in the image of its Creator" (Colossians 3:9–10). This passage contains a surprising truth and suggests a practical tool for Christian growth.

First, the surprising truth: the new self that we received in baptism is not a finished product. God is going to renew us progressively in his own image. The first time I read the above quote in Colossians, I said, "What?" Then I read the passage over and over again. The fact that the Lord intended to remake me to be like him startled and delighted me.

So in baptism we put on a new nature that God continues to develop and perfect. Our transformation is the work of the Holy Spirit, who replicates Christ's character in us and enables us to behave as he did when he lived on earth. Scripture calls these characteristics of Christ "fruit of the Spirit" and lists them as love, joy, peace, patience, kindness, goodness, trustfulness, gentleness, self-control, compassion, humility, mercy, and the like (see Galatians 5:22–23; Colossians 3:12). Note that these qualities define things that we do, not things that we feel. The Holy Spirit progressively renews us in the Lord's image not by inducing us to reproduce his feelings but by encouraging us to act as he did. Each fruit of the Spirit allows us to replace a bad behavior with a good one. We can substitute doing loving things for acting hatefully, making peace for fighting, restraining ourselves patiently for erupting angrily, and so on.

The practical tool suggested by Colossians 3 is a way to use the sign of the cross to help us replace evil conduct with the behaviors Christ exhibited. Let me give you some background before I tell you how it works.

The text employs the analogy of stripping off old clothes and putting on new ones to describe our transformation in Christ. The Fathers of the Church developed this theme, teaching that stripping off our old nature in baptism and putting on a new one was a participation in Christ's stripping at his crucifixion. In the early Church, candidates for baptism were stripped before their immersion, just as Christ was stripped at the cross. Addressing newly baptized Christians, St. Cyril of Jerusalem said:

> When you entered the baptistery, you took off your clothes as an image of putting off the old man with his deeds. Stripped naked, you were also imitating Christ, who was stripped naked on the cross. And by his nakedness he put off from himself the principalities and powers and fearlessly triumphed

over them on the cross. Since the evil powers once camped out in your members, you may no longer wear that old clothing. I am not speaking of your visible body, but the "old man" corrupted by its deceitful desires.[4]

As the newly baptized Christians emerged from the baptismal pool, they put on white garments, symbolizing that they had risen to a new life and put on Christ, who himself was clothed in glory at his resurrection. "Every one of you that has been baptised," said St. Paul, "has been clothed in Christ" (Galatians 3:27).

By now you have probably surmised how making the sign of the cross comes into play. We can regard it as our way of participating in Christ's stripping at the Crucifixion and his being clothed in glory at his resurrection. And we can use it to engage the grace of baptism to help us substitute fruit of the Spirit for acts of self-indulgence. We can trace the cross over our body while praying, "Lord, with this sign I strip off my evil tendencies, the residues of my old nature that still cling to me." Then we can sign ourselves again, praying, "O Holy Spirit, with this cross I put on Christ and ask you to help me behave as he did."

When I do this I get very specific. "Lord," I say as I cross myself, "In your name I strip off like dirty clothes my anger, my impatience, and my criticalness." Then I sign myself a second time, saying, "Lord, with this cross I put on Christ's restraint, his patience, and his compassion."

If my family and friends were to overhear me at these moments, they would breathe a great sigh of relief.

With this discussion of our victory over self-indulgence and transformation in the Spirit, we have completed our exploration of the sign of the cross. In the concluding chapter you will see the whole picture again and realize the advantages of adopting the sign as one of your regular spiritual disciplines.

CONCLUSION

Graces and Choices

Whene'er across this sinful flesh of mine
  I draw the Holy Sign,
All good thoughts stir within me, and renew
  Their slumbering strength divine;
Till there springs up a courage high and true
  To suffer and to do.

Venerable John Henry Newman (1801–90)[1]

If you bear on your forehead the sign of the humility of Jesus Christ,
bear in your heart the imitation of the humility of Jesus Christ.

St. Augustine (354–430)[2]

B LESSED ASSUNTA PALLOTTA (1878–1905), a simple girl from a poor Italian family, said that she joined the convent in order to become a saint. Her community, the Franciscan Missionaries of Mary, assigned her to work in the kitchen and on the farm. In 1904, they sent Assunta to serve at their mission in China. On the way there, she and her companions stopped in Bombay, India. She wrote the following about her experience there in a letter to her sisters back home:

> We saw four of these poor people bowing down
> in worship before a large stone painted red, and
> then dabbing their foreheads with some of the red
> varnish. I thought how they could put to shame
> some of us Christians who are so filled with human
> respect that we cannot even make the sign of the
> cross openly.[3]

I earnestly desire that Assunta's words will never apply to me or to any of you. I hope that as a result of reading this book you have felt freer to make the sign of the cross openly. I hope that you are imitating your Christian ancestors by signing yourself first thing in the morning and before you retire at night; when you eat and drink; when you leave the house and when you return; when you are walking, driving, riding a bus, and flying; at home, at school, at work, and at leisure. I hope that those of you who are athletes are making the sign to bless your time at the free-throw line or at home plate. I hope too that you are using the sign to bless your children, your relatives and friends, the sick, your pets, your home, and your stuff. In short, I hope you have begun to make the sign in all circumstances, as the Fathers of the Church prescribed.

We have been exploring the realties invoked by the sign of the cross. We have studied them as a way of recovering the power of this ancient prayer. Review them with me here so that they may be etched in your memory and available at your fingertips.

By making the sign of the cross:

- You confess your faith in the Blessed Trinity and in basic Christian doctrines, thus opening yourself to God. You ensure that you are praying to the God who created you, not one you created, and you call on God's name as a way of entering his presence and praying with Godpower.

- You choose to live the supernatural life you received when you died and rose with Christ at your baptism. You hold yourself to the fact that you have died to sin and so refuse to yield to it. You acknowledge your membership in the Body of Christ and expect the Holy Spirit to flow in you afresh.

- You affirm your decision to be Christ's disciple. You deny that you belong to yourself and you declare that all you are and have belongs to the Lord. You decide to follow him by embracing his teaching and obeying his commandments.

- You accept suffering as a normal part of the Christian life, and you realize that the Lord stays with you and supports you in your suffering. You embrace hardship and pain as a way of participating in Christ's suffering and of winning spiritual advantages for others.

- You remind the devil of Christ's victory, thus repelling him. You participate actively in Christ's battle against the devil. You claim the inviolability from spiritual enemies that you enjoy because you belong to Christ.

- You kill your self-indulgence and evil tendencies to sin. You strip off your old sinful nature and its bad behavior and clothe yourself with your new nature that the Lord is perpetually renewing in his image. And you acquire Christ's characteristics, the fruit of the Spirit.

Each time you make the sign of the cross you activate these realities. Occasionally as you sign yourself you may be aware of one or more of them. For example, your baptism or your discipleship may come to mind. Sometimes you may choose to focus specifically on one of them, such as accepting a hardship or refusing a temptation. But most of the time you cross yourself without thinking about any of these realities. As I have emphasized repeatedly, you must never make the sign of the cross casually or carelessly. You must always make it reverently and with faith.

I hope that it is now evident that making the sign of the cross is an easy spiritual discipline. What could be easier than touching your forehead, breast, and shoulders while praying in the Lord's name? You have at hand a simple gesture and prayer that opens you to a tremendous flow of graces. Making the sign is an act of faith that engages God's love for you and the spiritual power that he wants to release in you.

So in this regard the sign of the cross is easy, but you have also discovered in these pages that the sign sums up your Christian life and vocation, and because of that it is not so easy. It calls you to affirm hard choices, decisions that you have made at great personal cost. Making the sign says that you are holding yourself to these choices and in so doing are joining Christ at the cross. You are crucifying all the things that oppose the decisions you have made to embrace God's will. That's hard to do. But you have a stream of grace to support and sustain you in this effort.

Thus the sign of the cross opens us to graces that enable us to affirm our choices. With Venerable John Henry Newman we draw the holy sign across our sinful flesh "till there springs up a courage high and true / To suffer and to do." That's God's grace. With St. Augustine we mark our forehead with the sign of Christ's humility so that in our heart we might truly imitate his humility in holding fast to the decisions we have made, subordinating our will to God's will. That's our choice.

And by making the sign of the cross freely, like Blessed Assunta we just might become saints.

NOTES

Introduction: Recovering the Power of the Ancient Sign

1. A. A. Lambing, *The Sacramentals of the Holy Catholic Church* (New York: Benziger Brothers, 1892), 63.

2. Ibid., 75.

3. This story can be found at various Internet sites. See, for example, Luke Veronis, "The Sign of the Cross," http://www.incommunion.org/Cross.htm.

4. Herbert Thurston, "The Sign of the Cross," in *The Catholic Encyclopedia* (New York: The Universal Knowledge Foundation, 1907), 13:786.

5. Lambing, *Sacramentals,* 75.

6. *Catechism of the Catholic Church,* 2d ed. (Vatican City: Libreria Editrice Vaticana, 1997), section 1667.

7. Ibid., section 1670.

8. Bert Ghezzi, *Mystics and Miracles* (Chicago: Loyola Press, 2002), 53, 110.

1: A Short History of the Sign of the Cross

1. Herbert Thurston, "The Sign of the Cross," in *The Catholic Encyclopedia* (New York: The Universal Knowledge Foundation, 1907), 13:786–87. I modernized the medieval English of the text.

2. Martin Luther, *Luther's Little Instruction Book (The Small Catechism of Martin Luther)*, trans. Robert E. Smith (Project Wittenberg: http://www.iclnet.org/pub/resources/text/wittenberg/luther/little.book/web/book-appx.html), app. I.

3. St. Caesarius, *Sermons*, ed. Joseph Deferrari, The Fathers of the Church: A New Translation (Washington, D.C.: The Catholic University of America Press), 1:75.

4. Jean Daniélou, *The Bible and the Liturgy* (Ann Arbor, Mich.: Servant Books, 1979), 64.

5. Herbert Thurston, *Familiar Prayers: Their Origin and History*, selected and arranged by Paul Grosjean (Westminster, Md.: Newman Press, 1953), 1–2.

6. Ibid., 3.

7. Thurston, "Sign of the Cross," 786.

2: An Opening to God

1. Jean Joseph Gaume, *The Sign of the Cross in the Nineteenth Century*, translated by a Daughter of St. Joseph (Philadelphia: Peter F. Cunningham, 1873), 323.

2. *Catechism of the Catholic Church*, 2d ed. (Vatican City: Libreria Editrice Vaticana, 1997), section 184.

3. C. S. Lewis, *The Screwtape Letters* (New York: Macmillan, 1982), 11–12.

3: A Renewal of Baptism

1. Athanasius Braegelmann, *The Life and Writings of Saint Ildefonsus of Toledo* (Washington, D.C.: The Catholic University of America Press, 1942), 79.

2. Jean Daniélou, *The Bible and the Liturgy* (Ann Arbor, Mich.: Servant Books, 1979), 61.

3. Ibid. (my emphasis).

4. See the *Catechism of the Catholic Church*, 2d ed. (Vatican City: Libreria Editrice Vaticana, 1997), section 1262–65.

5. Adapted from St. Cyril of Jerusalem, *Catechetical Lectures*, lecture 20, no. 4, which can be found at *Nicene and Post-Nicene Fathers*, 2d ser., vol. 7, Christian Classics Ethereal Library at Calvin College (http://www.ccel.org/fathers2/NPNF2-07/TOC.htm).

6. Braegelmann, *Saint Ildefonsus of Toledo*, 79.

4: A Mark of Discipleship

1. Jean Joseph Gaume, *The Sign of the Cross in the Nineteenth Century*, translated by a Daughter of St. Joseph (Philadelphia: Peter F. Cunningham, 1873), 321.

2. Richard Oliver, "Saint Richard of Chichester," http://employees.csbsju.edu/roliver/richard.html, the Web site of the employees of College of St. Benedict (St. Joseph, Minn.) and St. John's University (Collegeville, Minn.).

3. Neal Lozano, *Unbound: A Practical Guide to Deliverance from Evil Spirits* (Grand Rapids, Mich.: Chosen Books, 2003), 54–57.

4. Adapted from Cyril, *Catechetical Lectures,* lecture 1, no. 2, which can be found at *Nicene and Post-Nicene Fathers,* 2d ser., vol. 7, Christian Classics Ethereal Library at Calvin College (http://www.ccel.org/fathers2/NPNF2-07/TOC.htm).

5. Adapted from St. Gregory Nazianzen, *Orations,* oration 40, no. 15, which can be found at *Nicene and Post-Nicene Fathers,* 2d ser., vol. 7, Christian Classics Ethereal Library at Calvin College (http://www.ccel.org/fathers2/NPNF2-07/TOC.htm).

6. Jean Daniélou, *The Bible and the Liturgy* (Ann Arbor, Mich.: Servant Books, 1979), 59.

7. See Austin Flannery, ed., *Vatican Council II: The Conciliar and Post Conciliar Documents,* new rev. ed. (Northport, N.Y.: Costello Publishing Company, 1992).

8. F. J. Sheed, *Theology and Sanity* (San Francisco: Ignatius Press, 1993); Edward D. O'Connor, C.S.C., *The Catholic Vision* (Huntington, Ind.: Our Sunday Visitor, 1992).

9. Sheed, *Theology and Sanity,* 7, 22–30.

5: An Acceptance of Suffering

1. Lactantius, *The Divine Institutes,* book 4, chapter 26, *Ante-Nicene Fathers: The Writings of the Fathers down to A.D. 325,* vol. 7, Christian Classics Ethereal Library at Calvin College (http://www.ccel.org/fathers2/ANF-07/TOC.htm).

2. Lucy Menzies, *Mirrors of the Holy: Ten Studies in Sanctity* (London: A. R. Mowbray, 1928), 303, 305.

3.   St. Ambrose, *The Principal Works of St. Ambrose, Nicene and Post-Nicene Fathers,* 2d ser., vol. 10, Christian Classics Ethereal Library at Calvin College (http://www.ccel.org/fathers2/NPNF2-10/TOC.htm).

6: A Defense against the Devil

1.   Adapted from St. Cyril of Jerusalem, *Catechetical Lectures,* lecture 13, no. 36, which can be found at *Nicene and Post-Nicene Fathers,* 2d ser., vol. 7, Christian Classics Ethereal Library at Calvin College (http://www.ccel.org/fathers2/NPNF2-07/TOC.htm).

2.   A. A. Lambing, *The Sacramentals of the Holy Catholic Church* (New York: Benziger Brothers, 1892), 63.

3.   An account of the St. Christopher legend may be found in various editions of *The Golden Legend* by Jacob of Voragine (ca. 1230–1298).

4.   John, Marquess of Bute, K. T., trans., *The Roman Breviary,* 4 vols. (Edinburgh and London: William Blackwood and Sons, 1908), 2, 352–53.

5.   Adapted from Cyril, *Catechetical Lectures,* lecture 3, no. 12.

7: A Victory over Self-Indulgence

1.   A. A. Lambing, *The Sacramentals of the Holy Catholic Church* (New York: Benziger Brothers, 1892), 65–66.

2.   Ibid., 66.

3.   Ibid., 62.

4. Adapted from St. Cyril of Jerusalem, *Catechetical Lectures*, lecture 20, no. 2, which can be found at *Nicene and Post-Nicene Fathers*, 2d ser., vol. 7, Christian Classics Ethereal Library at Calvin College (http://www.ccel.org/fathers2/NPNF2-07/TOC.htm).

Conclusion: Graces and Choices

1. Edmund Clarence Stedman, ed., *A Victorian Anthology, 1837–1895* (Cambridge: Riverside Press, 1895); Bartleby.com, 2003. http://www.bartleby.com/246/. August 7, 2003.

2. Jean Joseph Gaume, *The Sign of the Cross in the Nineteenth Century*, translated by a Daughter of St. Joseph (Philadelphia: Peter F. Cunningham, 1873), 324.

3. *The Theme Song of Assunta*, compiled by one of her sisters ([North Providence, R.I.]: Franciscan Missionaries of Mary, 1956), 122.

BIBLIOGRAPHY

Ante-Nicene Fathers: The Writings of the Fathers down to A.D. 325. Christian Classics Ethereal Library at Calvin College (www.ccel .org/fathers2).

Catechism of the Catholic Church. 2d ed. Vatican City: Libreria Editrice Vaticana, 1997.

Daniélou, Jean. *The Bible and the Liturgy.* Ann Arbor, Mich.: Servant Books, 1979.

————. *Primitive Christian Symbols.* London: Burns and Oates, 1964.

Gaume, Jean Joseph. *The Sign of the Cross in the Nineteenth Century.* Translated by a Daughter of St. Joseph. Philadelphia: Peter F. Cunningham, 1873.

Lambing, A. A. *The Sacramentals of the Holy Catholic Church.* New York: Benziger Brothers, 1892.

Lewis, C. S. *The Screwtape Letters.* New York: Macmillan, 1982.

Nicene and Post-Nicene Fathers. Christian Classics Ethereal Library at Calvin College (www.ccel.org/fathers2).

O'Connor, Edward D., C.S.C. *The Catholic Vision.* Huntington, Ind.: Our Sunday Visitor, 1992.

Richardson, Alan, ed. *A Theological Word Book of the Bible*. New York: Macmillan, 1950.

Sheed, F. J. *Theology and Sanity*. San Francisco: Ignatius Press, 1993.

Thurston, Herbert. *Familiar Prayers: Their Origin and History*. Selected and arranged by Paul Grosjean. Westminster, Md.: Newman Press, 1953.

———. "The Sign of the Cross." In vol. 13 of *The Catholic Encyclopedia*, 785–87. New York: The Universal Knowledge Foundation, 1907.

ACKNOWLEDGMENTS

Many thanks to Patricia Harrison Easton, Richard F. Easton, Mary Lou Ghezzi, Rev. Roger Prokop, William G. Storey, and Paul Thigpen, all of whom read *The Sign of the Cross* in manuscript and contributed suggestions that made it a much better book than I could have written without their help. I am also grateful to Fr. George Lane, S. J., Terry Locke, James Manney, Vinita Wright, Elysia Anderson, and all of my other friends at Loyola Press whose enthusiasm for the book is contagious. A special word of thanks to Heidi Hill, my wonderful editor, who made my sentences sing, caught many mistakes, and inspired me to write more personally about this very important topic. I am indebted to Joseph Durepos, my friend and agent, whose vision and encouragement impel me to be a better writer and a better person. And I extend my gratitude to the booksellers and distributors who make my books available, and to you, my readers, who buy them and, I hope, enjoy them and profit from them. I bless all of you with a big sign of the cross, "in the name of the Father, and of the Son, and of the Holy Spirit. Amen."